Send your Press Releases for Less and Get a Free Language Edition.

>> Increase your competitiveness with our packages

>> Be the news in every language

>> We take your news to local and global news media

>> Media contact and press release services

Media Monitoring, Analysis, and Measurement Services

>> TV and Radio News Monitoring

>> Online News and Social Media Monitoring

>> Monitor Competition

>> Measure PR & Marketing Effectiveness

>> Automate Daily, Weekly & Monthly Reports

Graphics and Communication Collateral Services

>> Print: Newsletters, Postcards, Calendar Design, Layout

>> Social Media: Campaign Management, Design

>> Website Design, Graphics

>> Video: Shooting, Producing, Editing

>> Advert/Media Buying Services

>> Printing Quotes

Editor's Comment

USA Oil and Gas Monitor

A RGT Media Communications Corp.

Energy Infrastructure and Energy independence- key factors to Economic Growth

The Gulf of Mexico area, both onshore and offshore, is one of the most important regions for energy resources and infrastructure. Gulf of Mexico federal offshore oil production accounts for 17 per cent of total U.S. crude oil production and federal offshore natural gas production in the Gulf accounts for 5 per cent of total U.S. dry production. Find our more analysis and the natural resources of states situated along the GOM, in addition, you will find out real time analysis of U.S. Gulf Coast Operable Refinery Capacity.

To bolster the USA energy infrastructure- that would lead to the nation's energy independence, President Trump revived the Keystone XL Pipeline, Dakota Access pipelines and advance energy Infrastructure Projects

In this edition- you will read the six mega-trends that could shape the future of energy. OPEC's JMMC erases every doubt of non-cooperation by member countries at first meeting- sees more market stability and less volatility since production cut is in effect.

PHMSA has placed on public inspection a final rule that amends the U.S. Hazardous Material Regulations HMR to maintain consistency with international regulations and standards. And lots more to read in this edition. Get Your Copy!

POGS Week '17 in partnership with City of Houston- Showcases "Must Have Technologies" for Oil and Gas companies, Midstream and Pipeline subsector and Downstream. The city of Houston mayor issued a proclamation affirming the conference and encouraging stake holders to attend the conference- The International Pipeline, Oil and Gas Safety Conference will take place in Houston Texas –March 14-16, 2017. Visit the event site for more details- www. oilandgassafetyconference.com

- Gloria Towolawi

Gloria Towolawi

Esther Coker

David Arhavbarien

Gloria Instead

Caleb Motinwo

Jewel Spring

Richard Godfirst

Contents

February 2017 • Issue 2

Gulf of Mexico- Energy Infrastructure Analysis in Real-Time

U.S. Gulf Coast Operable Refinery Capacity

Refiner	Refinery	State	(Barrels Per Calendar Day Capacity (2016)
Louisiana Gulf Coast Refining District			
Alon Refining Krotz Springs Inc	Krotz Springs	LA	80,000
Calcasieu Refining Co	Lake Charles	LA	89,000
Chalmette Refining LLC	Chalmette	LA	192,500
Chevron USA Inc	Pascagoula	MS	330,000
Citgo Petroleum Corp	Lake Charles	LA	427,800
ExxonMobil Refining & Supply Co	Baton Rouge	LA	502,500
Marathon Petroleum Company LLC	Garyville	LA	539,000
Motiva Enterprises LLC	Convent	LA	235,000
Motiva Enterprises LLC	Norco	LA	237,700
Phillips 66 Company	Belle Chasse	LA	247,000
Phillips 66 Company	Westlake	LA	260,000
Placid Refining Co	Port Allen	LA	75,000
Shell Chemical LP	Saraland	AL	91,575
Shell Oil Products U.S.	St. Rose	LA	45,000
Valero Refining New Orleans LLC	Norco	LA	215,000
Valero Energy Corp	Meraux	LA	125,000
Subtotal			3,692,075
Texas Gulf Coast Refining District			
Buckeye Texas Processing LLC	Corpus Christi	TX	46,250
Citgo Refining & Chemical Inc	Corpus Christi	TX	157,500
Deer Park Refining LTD Partnership	Deer Park	TX	285,500
ExxonMobil Refining & Supply Co	Baytown	TX	560,500
ExxonMobil Refining & Supply Co	Beaumont	TX	344,600
Flint Hills Resources LP	Corpus Christi	TX	295,630
Houston Refining LP	Houston	TX	263,776
Kinder Morgan Crude & Condensate	Galena Park	TX	84,000
Marathon Petroleum Company LLC	Galveston Bay	TX	459,000
Marathon Petroleum Company LLC	Texas City	TX	86,000
Motiva Enterprises LLC	Port Arthur	TX	603,000
Pasadena Refining Systems Inc	Pasadena	TX	112,229
Petromax Refining LLC	Houston	TX	25,000
Phillips 66 Company	Sweeny	TX	247,000
Premcor Refining Group Inc	Port Arthur	TX	335,000
Total Petrochemicals Inc	Port Arthur	TX	225,500
Valero Refining Co Texas LP	Corpus Christi	TX	293,000
Valero Refining Co Texas LP	Houston	TX	100,000
Valero Refining Co Texas LP	Texas City	TX	225,000
Subtotal			4,748,485
Total U.S. Gulf Coast Capacity			**8,440,560**
Total U.S. Capacity			**18,317,036**
U.S. Gulf Coast Share of U.S. Refinery Capacity			**46%**

The Gulf of Mexico area, both onshore and offshore, is one of the most important regions for energy resources and infrastructure. Gulf of Mexico federal offshore oil production accounts for 17 per cent of total U.S. crude oil production and federal offshore natural gas production in the Gulf accounts for 5 per cent of total U.S. dry production. Over 45 per cent of total U.S. petroleum refining capacity is located along the Gulf coast, as well as 51 per cent of total U.S. natural gas processing plant capacity.

Natural Gas Processing Plants along the Gulf of Mexico Coast, by Geographic Location

U.S. Gulf Coast Natural Gas Processing Plants by Geographic Location

Geographic Location	Number of Plants	Total Capacity (Bcf per day)	Total Flow (Bcf per day)	Percent Utilization	Average Capacity (MMcf per day)
Alabama	16	1	<1	42%	91
Louisiana	49	11	5	51%	219
Mississippi	4	2	<1	21%	468
Texas	166	21	16	74%	128
Total U.S. Gulf Coast	235	35	22	63%	150
Total U.S.	519	71	46	65%	137
U.S. Gulf Coast Share	**45%**	**50%**	**48%**		

Units: Billion cubic feet per day Bcf/d and million cubic feet per day MMcf/d.

Quick Facts on States Along the Gulf of Mexico Geographical Location

ALABAMA

- In 2014, Alabama ranked 17th in the nation in the number of producing natural gas wells.
- Mobile, Alabama was the third-largest seaport for exporting U.S. coal in 2015. Coking coal used in the steelmaking process accounted for 83 per cent of total exported coal.
- The three reactors at the Browns Ferry Nuclear Plant in Limestone County, Alabama have a combined generating capacity of 3,309 megawatts, second in capacity only to Arizona's Palo Verde nuclear plant.
- Alabama ranked eighth in 2015 in net electricity generation from renewable energy resources, including hydroelectric power. In 2015,

Alabama, U.S. Rankings

Consumption	
Total Energy per Capita	12
Expenditures	
Total Energy per Capita	18
Production	
Total Energy	16
Crude Oil	15
Natural Gas	16
Coal	15
Electricity	7
Prices	
Natural Gas	7
Electricity	21
Environment	
Carbon Dioxide Emissions	15

February 2017 • Issue 2

conventional hydroelectric power supplied 75 per cent of Alabama's generation from renewable resources.

- Alabama has the third-largest amount of timberland acreage among the Lower 48 states. In 2015, Alabama ranked fifth in the nation in electricity generation from biomass, much of it from wood and wood waste from the state's substantial forest products industry.

FLORIDA

- Geologists believe there may be large crude oil and natural gas deposits in the federal Outer Continental Shelf off Florida's western coast.
- Florida was second only to Texas in 2015 in net electricity generation, and third in the nation in electricity consumption, behind Texas and California.
- Renewable energy accounted for 2.3 per cent of Florida's total net electricity generation in 2015. Nearly nine-tenths of that renewable power came from biomass.
- Five-sixths of the natural gas consumed in Florida is used to generate electricity, and natural gas fuels nearly two-thirds of Florida's net electricity generation.
- Florida's Martin generating station is the only concentrating solar thermal plant east of the Rocky Mountains and produced one-fourth of the state's net solar generation in 2015.
- Electricity accounts for 90 per cent of the site energy consumed by Florida households, and the annual electricity expenditures of $1,900 are 40 per cent higher than the U.S. average, per EIA's Residential Energy Consumption Survey.

LOUISIANA

- The Henry Hub in Erath, Louisiana, where 13 major pipeline systems interconnect, is the delivery point for the benchmark natural gas futures contract traded on the New York Mercantile Exchange.
- With 18 operating petroleum refineries, Louisiana is, as of January 2016, second only to Texas in both total and operating refinery capacity.
- The Louisiana Offshore Oil Port LOOP is the only U.S. port capable of berthing Ultra Large Crude Carriers, the largest ocean-going crude oil tankers.
- In early 2016, the first large-scale LNG export terminal in the Lower 48 states opened at Sabine Pass, Louisiana. The only other U.S. LNG tanker export port is in Nikiski, Alaska.
- In 2014, Louisiana ranked first among the states in total energy consumption per capita, primarily because of the state's industrial sector, which includes many refineries and petrochemical plants.

MISSISSIPPI

- The Gulf Liquefied Natural Gas terminal at Pascagoula, Mississippi was designed to send imported natural gas by pipeline to users throughout the South. Because of changing market conditions, plans to add liquefaction and export capabilities are being pursued.
- As of January 2015, the Pascagoula oil refinery is the 11th-largest refinery by capacity in the United States. The Pascagoula refinery can process about 330,000 barrels of crude oil per calendar day.
- The 1,443 megawatt Grand Gulf Nuclear Station, near Port Gibson along the Mississippi River, is the largest single-unit nuclear power plant in the nation. In 2015, it generated 18 per cent of Mississippi's electricity.
- Mississippi's one ethanol plant can produce 54 million gallons of

Florida, U.S. Rankings

Consumption	
Total Energy per Capita	47
Expenditures	
Total Energy per Capita	51
Production	
Total Energy	30
Crude Oil	23
Natural Gas	28
Coal	--
Electricity	2
Prices	
Natural Gas	4
Electricity	36
Environment	
Carbon Dioxide Emissions	6

Louisiana, U.S. Rankings

Consumption	
Total Energy per Capita	1
Expenditures	
Total Energy per Capita	3
Production	
Total Energy	8
Crude Oil	9
Natural Gas	5
Coal	17
Electricity	15
Prices	
Natural Gas	46
Electricity	51
Environment	
Carbon Dioxide Emissions	7

Mississippi, U.S. Rankings

Consumption	
Total Energy per Capita	16
Expenditures	
Total Energy per Capita	11
Production	
Total Energy	34
Crude Oil	13
Natural Gas	20
Coal	18
Electricity	28
Prices	
Natural Gas	46
Electricity	45
Environment	
Carbon Dioxide Emissions	32

biofuel annually, equal to 0.34 per cent of total U.S. ethanol production capacity.
- Mississippi generated nearly 2.3 per cent of its electricity from renewable energy resources during 2015, with wood and wood waste accounting for almost all the state's renewable electricity generation.

TEXAS
- Texas was the leading crude oil-producing state in the nation in 2015 and exceeded production levels even from the federal offshore areas.
- As of January 2016, the 29 petroleum refineries in Texas had a capacity of over 5.4 million barrels of crude oil per day and accounted for 30 per cent of total U.S. refining capacity.
- Texas accounted for over 27 per cent of U.S. marketed natural gas production in 2015, making it the leading natural gas producer among the states.
- Texas leads the nation in wind-powered generation capacity with more than 18,500 megawatts; in 2014 and 2015, Texas wind turbines produced more electricity than the state's two nuclear plants.
- Texas is the nation's largest producer of lignite coal. About 40 per cent of the coal burned for electricity generation in Texas is lignite.
- The average annual electricity cost per Texas household is $1,801, among the highest in the nation; the cost is like other warm weather states like Florida, per EIA's Residential Energy Consumption Survey.

Texas, U.S. Rankings

Consumption	
Total Energy per Capita	6
Expenditures	
Total Energy per Capita	5
Production	
Total Energy	1
Crude Oil	1
Natural Gas	1
Coal	7
Electricity	1
Prices	
Natural Gas	8
Electricity	39
Environment	
Carbon Dioxide Emissions	1

February 2017 • Issue 2

Understanding LNG- Recent Pricing Issues

Given the volatility and significant variations in regional gas pricing over the last few years, both LNG sellers and LNG buyers are becoming increasingly focused on how to develop gas pricing mechanisms which give sellers a revenue which reflects the global value of their product, in a manner that will support project development. These pricing mechanisms also provide buyers with a market clearing price, which will enable them to supply gas to their customers at a competitive rate. With the increasing power of buyers in the currently over-supplied market, new pricing mechanisms are emerging which give the buyer a choice or mix of pricing indices. This new flexibility is sometimes coupled with short-term volume and destination flexibility, with the ability to turn back cargoes that are priced at what the buyer may consider an uncompetitive level.

These increasingly complex price-and-volume provisions are leading sellers to more complex hedging and risk management strategies. New pricing provisions are also supporting the LNG aggregator business model, where an intermediary, either an IOC or an LNG trading entity, takes on the role of accommodating both buyer and seller pricing concerns and manages a portfolio of gas sources and destinations to appropriately manage risk.

LNG pricing formulas are evolving now from pure oil-linked pricing to pure gas-linked pricing, although the full evolutionary process is still underway. Thus, there are various mixed pricing formulas in use now, including pricing techniques that modulate fluctuations in oil pricing, such as an "S" curve which bends the percentage of a crude price at extreme highs and lows.

Another consideration in pricing is the emergence of 'pricing review' clauses in LNG SPAs, where the LNG price can be examined and changed at periodic intervals if specified market conditions are triggered. While the intent of these clauses is to preserve a link between a long-term contract and the actual market pricing, such clauses can be very contentious and lead to disputes between sellers and buyers.

Natural gas prices in 2017 and 2018 are expected to rise- EIA

In the meantime, in its January 2017 Short-Term Energy Outlook STEO, EIA expects the Henry Hub natural gas spot price to average $3.55 per million British thermal units MMBtu in 2017 and $3.73/MMBtu in 2018, both higher than the 2016 average of $2.51/MMBtu. Higher prices in 2017 and 2018 reflect natural gas consumption and exports exceeding supply and imports, leading to lower average inventory levels.

The confidence interval range for natural gas prices is a market-derived range that reflects trading in New York Mercantile Exchange NYMEX futures markets and is not directly based on EIA's supply and demand estimates. The values for the upper confidence interval increase during the winter months compared with the rest of the year, which reflects the higher probability of an increase in natural gas consumption for space heating use because of colder weather. By February 2018, the 95% confidence interval ranges from $1.78/MMBtu to $7.22/MMBtu.

In 2016, the annual average Henry Hub natural gas price was the lowest since 1999 because of a very mild winter that left natural gas inventories at a record high for the end of March. However, high natural gas use for electricity generation during the summer and declining production contributed to Henry Hub natural gas prices rising from an average of $2.00/MMBtu in the first quarter of 2016 to an average of $2.88/MMBtu in the third quarter of 2016. Cold weather across much of the northern United States in mid-December led to an increase in demand for space heating, much of which is provided by natural gas, contributing to natural gas inventories ending the month below the five-year average. Thus, Henry Hub spot prices increased to a monthly average of $3.59/MMBtu in December, the first month in which prices averaged above $3.00/MMBtu since December 2014.

In 2017, Henry Hub prices are expected to remain near the levels in December 2016, leaving annual average prices in 2017 higher than those in 2016. Prices are expected to be higher again in 2018. The higher prices are the result of forecasted consumption and exports exceeding forecasted production and imports, which implies that the difference will be supplied from inventories. Because natural gas use for space heating in

the residential and commercial sectors depends significantly on winter weather, any significant discrepancy between weather assumptions used in the forecast and actual weather could significantly affect both consumption and prices.

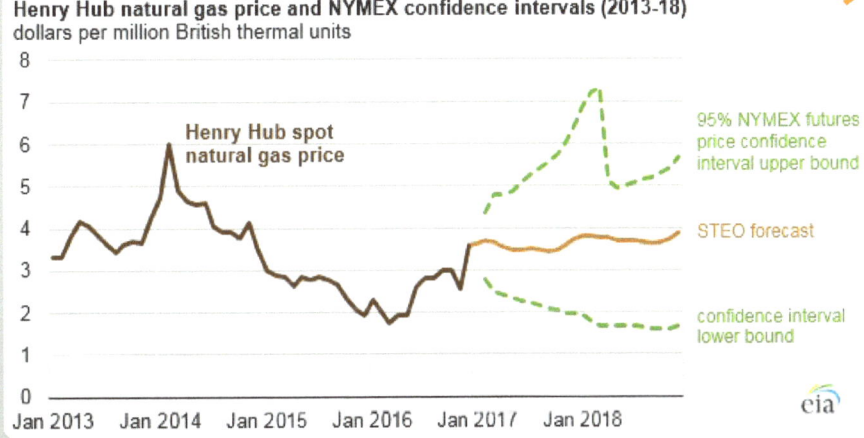

Henry Hub natural gas price and NYMEX confidence intervals (2013-18)
dollars per million British thermal units

Henry Hub spot natural gas price

95% NYMEX futures price confidence interval upper bound

STEO forecast

confidence interval lower bound

Background

As opposed to crude oil, LNG does not feature a harmonized global price. In contracts, the price of LNG is segmented into regional markets, the main ones being:

- the Asian market, Japan, Korea, and China, with the Japan Customs cleared Crude price index

- the European market with the National Balancing Point price index

- the North American market with the Henry Hub price index.

LNG pricing has historically been tied to crude oil, as the replacement fuel to natural gas. Pricing into Japan and much of Asia was based on a percentage of the price of Japan Customs-cleared Crude JCC, which is the average price of custom-cleared crude oil imports into Japan as reported in customs statistics; nicknamed the Japanese Crude Cocktail. As an example, a pricing formula may be "LNG price = JCC x 0.135" where JCC is further defined as the previous three monthly averages of JCC priced in yen and converted into US dollars. In Europe, Brent has been favored in oil linked LNG pricing formulas. LNG pricing in parts of Europe and in North America have relatively recently been tied to readily available natural gas indices. In Europe, a main index is NBP or National Balancing Point, a virtual trading location for the sale and purchase and exchange of UK natural gas. In North America, a main index is Henry Hub, a distribution hub in South Louisiana which lends its name to the pricing

February 2017 • Issue 2

point for traded natural gas futures contracts.

LNG Reference Market Price

As noted in the previous section, LNG pricing is following the global trend that has been underway for many decades, whereby instead of being priced relative to oil, it is starting to be priced based on a variety of established and emerging global reference prices. This is generally referred to as "gas-on-gas" pricing as it is a measure of the relative supply and demand in natural gas markets, quite independently of whether the oil market is in balance or not. From an economist's point of view, this would be the established way to set the appropriate market clearing price for a globally traded commodity.

The US market

The historical rationale for gas reference pricing emerged from the development of a liquids wholesale market in the US, with exchange-traded futures contracts to support a pricing mechanism that was not vulnerable to undue influence from a single buyer or seller, and was derived from a transparent, market-based mechanism. Historically, natural gas prices were fixed by the government, but in 1992, the Federal Energy Regulatory Commission FERC issued its Order 636. Prices were decontrolled and interstate natural gas pipeline companies were required to split-off any nonregulated merchant sales functions from their regulated transportation functions. This unbundling of gas contract pricing and transportation contract pricing meant that exchange-traded gas contracts, based on Henry Hub and other secondary hubs, were established, and the industry moved to market-based indices for pricing purposes.

The European market

In Europe, this same trend was first established in the UK, following gas market deregulation in the mid-1990s, and the emergence of National Balancing Point NBP pricing, which, though like Henry Hub, is not a physical place. In Continental Europe, the so-called Title Transfer Facility TTF has now become an equally dependable mechanism for long-term pricing, though Southern Europe is still transitioning to a mechanism of gas-on-gas pricing, as new hubs start to emerge.

The Asia-Pacific market

The first signs that a new pricing basis was emerging for the Asia-Pacific region occurred in the early 2010s with the signing of Henry Hub-based LNG tolling contracts. At the time, buying gas in the US and paying a tolling fee to put it through one of the emerging LNG liquefaction facilities, represented a lower landed price in Japan and other SE Asian countries, compared to traditionally oil-priced gas. Several attempts are being made to establish a pricing index for the Asia-Pacific market, including the so-called JKM index, Japan-Korea-Marker, and the Singapore Gas Exchange SGX spot price index known as SLiNG, which is intended to represent an exchange-traded futures market for LNG based on gas being traded at or around the Singapore LNG facilities. At the time of writing, no index exists that is considered sufficiently dependable for use on long-term contract pricing.

Current developments

The LNG sector has been relatively slow to move away from oil-based pricing. There are many reasons for this, but the main brake on pricing change for LNG has been the lack of availability of a reliable, transparent pricing reference for gas, like Henry Hub or NBP, in the Asia-Pacific region, which accounts for about two-thirds of LNG consumption. The other feature of LNG, compared to pipeline gas, is that it is bought and sold in single ship-borne cargoes, instead of being commingled within a pipeline system, and this too has tended to slow down the development of gas on gas mechanisms. In Europe, over the last decade, most traded gas has now migrated from oil-based to gas on gas based pricing, and some commentators believe that gas-on-gas based pricing will gradually replace oil-based index pricing, particularly as new LNG projects bring additional LNG into the global markets.

An increasing number of African countries are considering moving to LNG imports, or establishing relatively smaller scale projects. Because these are under development and/or negotiations, no pricing has been established yet.

Price Indexation

Natural gas may be sold indexed to the price of certain alternative fuels such as crude oil, coal and fuel oil. The natural gas feedstock prices into the LNG plants are sometimes indexed on the full revenue stream of the LNG plant including LPG and propane plus other gas liquids, as in the case of the 2009 amendment of the NLNG contract in Nigeria. Such a pricing mechanism is markedly different from the one found in traded gas markets, where price is determined solely by gas demand and supply at market areas or "hubs".

In the United Kingdom, around 60 per cent of the gas is sold at the National Balancing Point NBP price and the rest at an oil index price based on old long-term contracts. The oil-indexed and hub-priced contracts co-exist.

On the European continent, the case is different. Oil-indexed contracts dominate, with hardly any hub-priced long-term contracts. The continental markets are mainly supplied on a long-term take-or-pay basis. However, several short-to-medium contracts do exist which are either fully or partially hub-priced.

Spot and Short-Term Markets

In recent years, the LNG markets have seen the emergence of a growing spot and short-term LNG market, which generally includes spot contracts and contracts of less than four years. Short-term and spot trade allows divertible or uncommitted LNG to go to the highest value market in response to changing market conditions. The short-term and spot market began to emerge in the late 1990s-early 2000s. The LNG spot and short term market grew from virtually zero before 1990, to 1 per cent in 1992, to 8 per cent in 2002. In 2006, nine countries were active spot LNG exporters and 13 countries were spot LNG importers.

Due to divergent prices between the markets in recent years, the short-term LNG market has grown rapidly. By 2010, the short-term and spot trade had jumped to account for 18.9 per cent of the world LNG trade. In 2011, the spot and short-term again recorded strong growth, reaching 61.2 MTPA 994 cargoes and more than 25 per cent of the total LNG trade. Asia attracted almost 70 per cent of the global spot and short-term volumes primarily due to Japan's increased LNG need following the March 2011 Fukushima disaster, which took Japan's nuclear reactors offline. This lost power was replaced with LNG. Spot and short-

term LNG imports into Korea almost doubled 10.7 MTPA and almost tripled for China and India with both countries importing a combined 6.5 MTPA of LNG.

By the end of 2011, twenty-one countries were active spot LNG exporters and 25 countries were spot LNG importers. The growing number of countries looking to participate in the spot market is indicative of the increased desire for flexibility to cope with market changes, unforeseen events such as Fukushima, as well as the increased number of countries now participating in the LNG markets.

In 2015, global LNG trade accounted for 245.2 MTPA, a 2.5 per cent increase vs. 2014. There are now 34 countries importing LNG and 19 countries that export LNG. Approximately 28 per cent of global LNG volumes 68.4 MTPA were traded on a spot or short-term basis.

The following chart shows the growing importance of spot and short-term sales in global LNG trade:

Spot and Short Term* Vs Total LNG Trade *

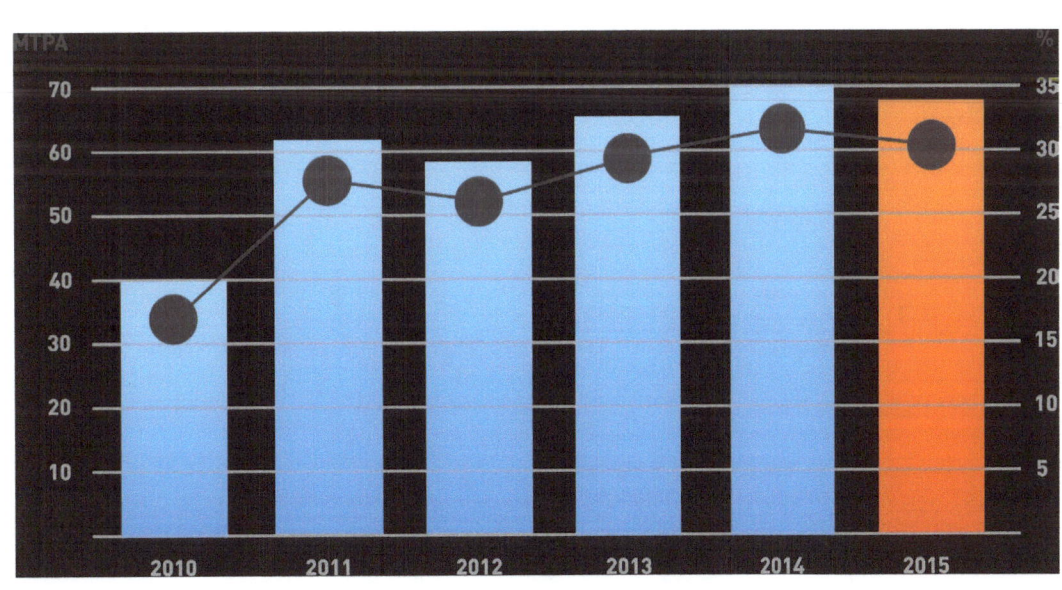

*short-term trade denotes trades under contracts of a duration of 4 years or less.

Rig Count Overview and Summary Count

Area	Last Count	Count	Change from Prior Count	Date of Prior Count	Change from Last Year	Date of Last Year's Count
U.S.	20 January 2017	694	+35	13 January 2017	+57	22 January 2016
Canada	20 January 2017	342	+27	13 January 2017	+92	22 January 2016
International	December 2016	929	+4	November 2016	-166	December 2015

USA Oil and Gas Monitor
A RGT Media Communications Corp.

SUBSCRIPTION FORM

First Name _____ Middle _____ Last _____

Current Job Title _____ Job Title Code _____

Company Name _____

Preferred Mailing Address - (Circle One)

    Business   Residence

Street _____ (No PO Boxes Please)

City _____ State _____ Zip _____

Country _____

Day Phone _____ If outside U.S., include country code. (ex: 000-000-000-0000)

Fax _____ Email _____

Form Instructions:

Email completed form to subscribe@usaoilandgasmonitor.com or mail form with check to the address below.

RGT Media Communications Corp.
10777 Westheimer Road #1100
Houston Texas 77042

1 Year Digital Subscription

For non-Texas subscribers - $119.88

Subscribers living in Texas – pays $119.88 plus 8.25% state tax $9.89 = $129.77

1 Year Print Subscription

For non-Texas subscribers - $144

Please add shipping cost and multiply by 12 (for example $1.67 x12) = 20.04

Subscribers living in Texas – pays $144 plus 8.25% state tax $11.88= $155.88

Please add shipping cost and multiply by 12 (for example $1.67 x12) = 20.04

Shipping Cost (calculated by weight)

Circle choice from the following option and add to the subscription cost

First Class 1- 5 business/days = $1.67

Fedex Shipping 1-3 business/days= $6.40

USPS Priority 1-3 business/days= $3.56

International First Class 1-7 business/days= $12.44

You can also pay for subscription online by visiting our website:
www.usaoilandgasmonitor.com/subscribe
Wire transfer, call Jewel Spring, 832-486-0095 for any questions.

Payment Method

Card Type (circle one)

Amex   Visa   Master   Discovery

Card No.

_____

Expiration Date

_____

CSV No.

_____

Name on Card

_____

By Check

Check No.

_____

OPEC's JMMC sees More Market Stability and Less Volatility Since Production Cut Is in Effect

OPEC's 1st Meeting of the Joint Ministerial Monitoring Committee JMMC press conference at OPEC Secretariat in Vienna, Austria. The JMMC is composed of three OPEC Member Countries – Algeria, Kuwait and Venezuela, and two non-OPEC countries – the Russian Federation and Oman. The Committee agreed to full and timely conformity to the agreement with the following stipulations:

- The OPEC Secretariat will present a monthly production data report on OPEC Member Countries' crude oil and of the participating non-OPEC oil liquid production to the JMMC by the 17th of each upcoming month.

- Evaluation of conformity to the respective country production adjustment will be based on production data only.

- Each of the five member countries of the JMMC will nominate one technical contact person, to form a Joint Technical Committee JTC, which shall include the Presidency of the OPEC Conference and shall assist the respective Ministers. The JTC will regularly cooperate with the OPEC Secretariat in preparing the monthly report for the JMMC and meet monthly before submitting their report to the JMMC.

- The JMMC will communicate monthly, after the 17th of each upcoming month, to consider the reports presented by the JTC and the OPEC Secretariat, as well as meet after the 17th of March 2017 and before the OPEC Conference in May 2017.

- The JMMC will issue a monthly press release on the progress towards the implementation of the OPEC 171st Ministerial Conference Decision and the Declaration of Cooperation.

- The JMMC will report to the Conference on the effect of the implementation of the OPEC 171st Ministerial Conference Decision and the Declaration of Cooperation on the market.

JMMC background and press conference Q and A excerpt below.

HE Barkindo: Mr. Chairman, Mr. Co-chair, Excellencies, distinguished members of the media, it is my honor and privilege to formally introduce to you our chairman, the newly appointed Minister of Oil of the state of Kuwait, His Excellency Issam Almarzooq, who has just, together with his colleague, His Excellency Alexander Novak, Russia's Energy Minister, successfully chaired the inaugural meeting of this historic committee coming out of a historic declaration of OPEC and non-OPEC on December 10th. This marking the commencement of the implementation phase of this historic decision.

HE Mohammad Sanusi Barkindo, OPEC Secretary General

So, I will hand over the floor to him to introduce his fellow colleague's members of the committee, whom I believe do not need any introduction, except the Minister of Venezuela, Nelson Martinez, a veteran of the industry who is not new to this industry, but I will leave that to the chairman to introduce his colleagues. Welcome. The chairman.

HE Almarzooq: I am glad to announce that we have concluded our first inaugural meeting of the Joint Ministerial Monitoring Committee JMMC that was established by the Vienna December 10th Agreement. I am glad to introduce the members of this committee, the co-chair, His Excellency the Minister of Russia, Mr. Alexander Novak, His Excellency the Minister of Venezuela, Dr. Nelson Martinez, His Excellency the Minister of Algeria Dr. Noureddine Boutarfa, and His Excellency Minister of Oman Dr. Mohammed Rumaihi, and the out-going president of the OPEC Conference, Dr. Mohammed Al-Sada, Minister of Oil, Qatar.

Our meeting was concluded with a total agreement of the mechanism of the monitoring of the OPEC December 10 agreement and also agreed on the forming of a Joint Technical Committee that will raise the reports that will be compiled in cooperation with the OPEC Data Center to the ministers of this esteemed committee; and agreed on the times that the committee will convene and communicate during the next five months to discuss the reports that will be issued by the OPEC Secretariat in cooperation with the Joint Technical Committee.

The Joint Technical Committee will be formed by the

five members of this committee. Technical persons will be nominated from each country, in addition to the presidency of the OPEC, as well. Our next meeting will be convened after the 17th of March, after the release of the February data. We will convene, hopefully, initially we agreed to convene in Kuwait and we will meet in Kuwait during the second half of March.

The third meeting for this committee will be held ahead of the OPEC Conference, that will be held in Vienna in May. We will hold our committee's meeting before that date.

JMMC Erases Every Doubt of Non-Cooperation by Member Countries at First Meeting

HE Novak: Excellencies, dear ladies and gentlemen, representatives of the press welcome. I would like to say that we have just concluded the inaugural meeting of the Monitoring Committee, which has been formed as per the result of the Declaration of Cooperation signed on the 10th of December between OPEC and non-OPEC countries.

- The two goals of this meeting were: the assessment of the implementation of a declaration of cooperation from December and

- Discuss the mechanisms and the framework of the Monitoring Committee.

As the first part is concerned, I can say with confidence that we are very happy to see the success of the joint action and effort by OPEC and non-OPEC countries as far as the efforts in the stabilizing the market are concerned.

OPEC and non-OPEC countries show very good level of conformity and commitments to the agreements

Based on our data and what we are seeing is a very good level of conformity and commitments to the agreements. At this point, we have no reason to doubt that there would be any significant deviations here. We believe the countries are very committed to this common cause. The results which were observed starting from the beginning of the year are exceeding our expectations. Many countries are going beyond what has been agreed, working in accordance with the spirits of declaration of the letter.

I would like to express my sincere gratitude to the

OPEC and non-OPEC Ministers pictured with HE Barkindo at the OPEC Secretariat

ministers and to the countries which are participating in the agreement and to all the ministers and my colleagues present here at this inaugural meeting.

I would also like to say thank you for the efforts which the countries are exerting not only to help stabilize the market, but also to support sustainable and stable development of the global economy. While assessing the market today, we are indeed seeing more stability in the market. We are starting to see inventory draws accelerating, but what is also very important is that we are starting to see a decline in volatility of the oil price.

The mechanism and the framework of the Monitoring Committee

- We have discussed in detail the mechanism and the framework of the Monitoring Committee. We have agreed that to complement the efforts of the Joint Ministerial Monitoring Committee, a technical committee will be created, which would consist of technical representatives of all the countries represented in the Ministerial Committee, as well as a representative of Saudi Arabia as the presidency of OPEC.

- The technical committee would be working in real time. It would be communicating and meeting monthly, working on reports and assessment of the situation, which would later be presented to the Ministerial Monitoring Committee and to all the participating countries.

- The Ministerial Committee itself would meet on

bimonthly basis and we expect to meet twice before the next OPEC Conference.

Press Q and A

HE Almarzooq: I think we can open the floor for question and answers. Please state your name and to whom you would like to direct your question. Thank you.

Bloomberg: Can you tell us exactly how much of the 1.8 million barrel a day joint cut has been made so far? Does the committee have a view at this point whether there will be any need to extend the agreement once it expires in six months' time? Thank you.

HE Almarzooq: As explained earlier, the data for each month will be presented to the Joint Technical Committee on the 17th of each month. They will review the data and they will raise their report to the Joint Ministerial Monitoring Committee. So as of today, we have not seen any data. We are monitoring the market through the data coming from OPEC Data Center. The results so far are very promising. I cannot give an exact number. This will be revealed next month when we review the monthly report. A press release will be issued after that.

As for the extension of another six months, we will review the data at the end of the six months' period and we will meet in Vienna in May. We will consider the extension if required. Thank you.

continued on page 19

POGS March 2017

Organized by:

RGT MEDIA
COMMUNICATIONS CORP.

The Intl Pipeline Oil and GAS Safety Conference and Exhibition

March 14-16, 2017 Houston Texas USA

Pipeline Integrity | **Emission Reduction** | **Well Control** | **Oil and Gas Transportation** | **Chemical Extraction**

Connecting Supplier with Procurement Teams

Exhibition
200+
Exhibitors Expected

Attendance
2000+
Attendees Expected

Goal

Improve safety in the entire value chain of the oil and gas industry not limited to the well heads but distribution chains, transportation and supply chain.

Exhibit@ P O G S Safety Tech

P O G S Safety Tech provides international and local energy companies who operate across the up, mid and downstream sectors of the oil &gas supply chain with a B2B platform to meet and influence highly-focused International decision-makers and buyers.

Who is Attending?

Take Advantage of Early Registration- Register Now @

http://www.oilandgassafetyconference.com
registration/online-registration/

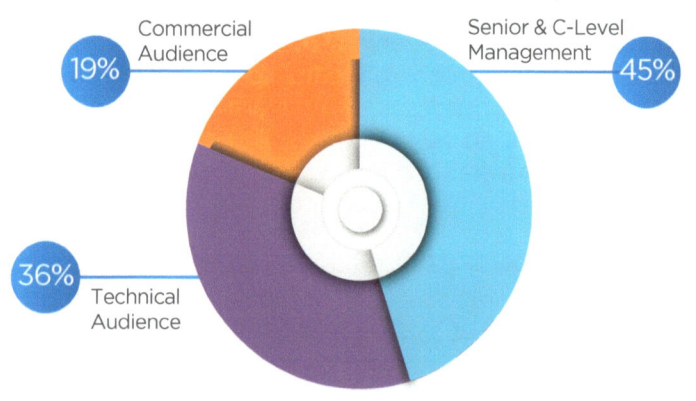

- 19% Commercial Audience
- 45% Senior & C-Level Management
- 36% Technical Audience

Who is Exhibiting?

SHOWFLOOR IS Selling Very Fast
RESERVED Today

http://www.oilandgassafetyconference.com/
booth-registeration/

Official Media Partner

USA Oil and Gas Monitor
A RGT Media Communications Corp.

For further details visit website @
http://oilandgassafetyconference.com
or call +1-832-664-0618

The International Pipeline, Oil and Gas Safety Conference

POGS
Intl Pipeline, Oil and Gas
Safety Conference &
Exhibition

POGS March 14-16, 2017   www.oilandgassafetyconference.com

Goals

This conference seeks to *address process safety issues* in the upstream, midstream and downstream subsectors of the industry; with special focus on well control safety, process safety, pipeline safety, and new regulatory impact.

To help improve operational excellence in the various communities where the industry operates- emerging technologies, leak detection and prevention technologies, emission reduction technologies, compliance audit, best practices to reduce risks and hazards, and improve the overall operational safety is the focal point of this conference.

To help meet these goals - are the speakers and participating companies

Brady Austin
QHSE Service Line Owner Lloyd's Register

Mothusi Pahl
Vice President- Alphabet Energy Inc.

Vincent Higgins
Chairman and CEO Optech4D Inc

Hunter Hawa
Global EHS Director for PSRG

Robert Miller
Regulatory Compliance Specialist, Veriforce

W. Duncan Welder IV
RISC's Director of Client Services

Shoshi Kaganovsky
CEO and founder of SensoLeak

Alexis Vitone
President, AvA Excellence in Business Strategies & HSE, LLC

Tom Meek
Director of Compliance, Veriforce

Keith J. Coyle
Shareholder, Babst Calland

Mark A. Hernandez
President of Multiply Leadership

Rixio Medina
Director of Business Development for the Board of Certified Safety Professionals

Registration Fee - $500

Register Today for this all important industrial conference

Fill out this form email form to: *registration@oilandgassafetyconference.com*

Or mail form with check to the address below.

Mail and make check payable to: *RGT Media Communications Corp.*   *10777 Westheimer Street, #1100 Houston Texas 77042*

Payment Method -Card type- Amex, Visa, Master, Discovery (circle one)

Card No: _____   Expiration Date: _____   Name on card: _____   By Check Check No: _____

First Name: _____   Last Name: _____

Your Preferred Mailing Address - (Circle One) Business/ Residence

Job Title: _____   Company Name : _____   Street : _____

(No PO Boxes Please) City : _____   State: _____   Country: _____   Zip/Postal Code: ____

Day Phone: _____   Fax: _____   E-mail: _____

cut here ✂

Program Agenda Break Down

Pipeline Safety- Leak Detection and Prevention Tech

Shoshi Kaganovsky - CEO and founder of SensoLeak

Emerging Technologies - Leveraging Virtual and Augmented Reality Technologies for Midstream & pipeline industries

Vincent Higgins - Chairman and CEO Optech4D Inc

Best Practices- Avoiding risks and hazards/ Competency-Based Training Program

Alexis Vitone- President - AvA Excellence in Business Strategies & HSE, LLC

Brady Austin - QHSE Service Line Owner- Lloyd's Register

W. Duncan Welder IV - RISC's Director of Client Services

Motivational Speaker

Mark A. Hernandez - President Multiply Leardership

Process Safety

Hunter Hawa - Global EHS Director for PSRG

PHMSA Regulations

Keith J. Coyle - Shareholder- Attorney at Law - Babst Calland

Emission Reduction Technology- Converting Flares to Power Gen

Mothusi Pahl - Vice President-Alphabet Energy Inc.

Compliance Audit- Federal/State codes and OQ NPRM

Tom Meek - Director of Compliance, Veriforce

Robert Miller - Regulatory Compliance Specialist, Veriforce

Rixio Medina - Director of Business Development for the Board of Certified Safety Professionals

---

Supporting Organization
Pennsylvania Independent Oil and Gas Association
PIOGA

Official Media Partner
USA Oil and Gas Monitor

Member Organization
Independent Petroleum Association of America
IPAA

POGS
Intl Pipeline, Oil and Gas
Safety Conference &
Exhibition

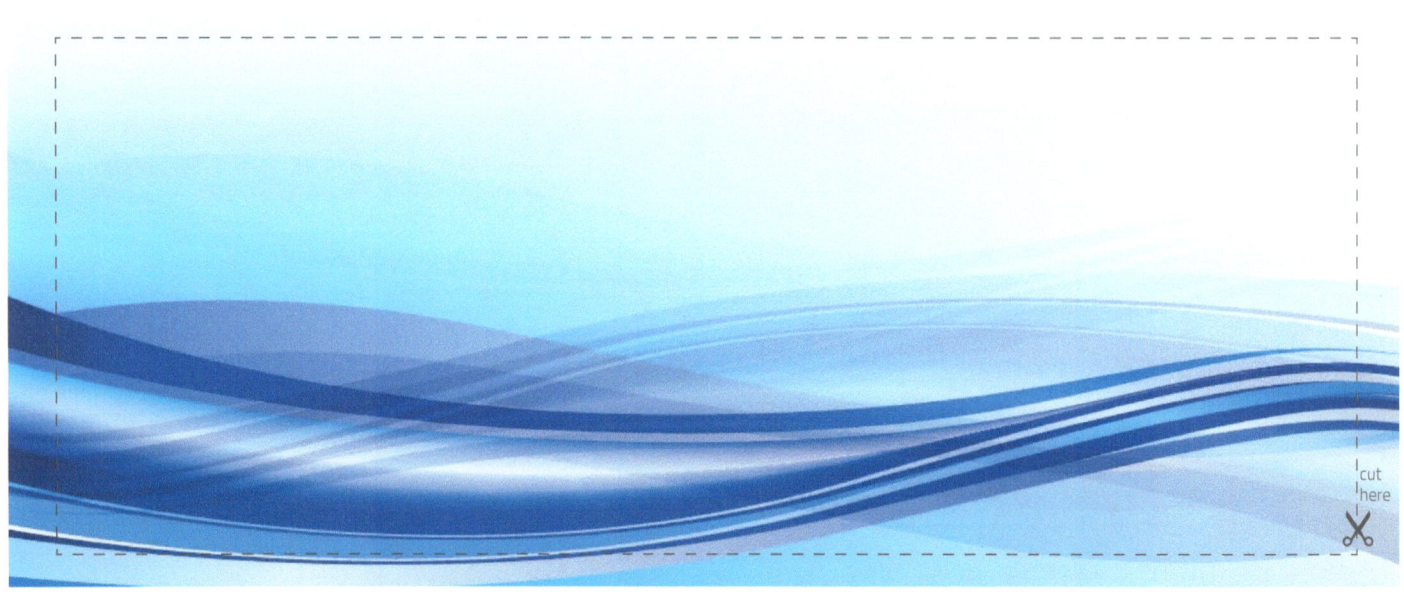

cut
here

continued from page 15

Press: How will the monitoring process work and what are the parameters that would be considered?

HE Novak: The monitoring process would be based on data received from many reputable international agencies, which would include EIA, IAEA, IHS, and other agencies.

We have agreed that each country participating in the agreement would nominate one technical person who would be responsible for submitting data to OPEC and this also includes representatives of non-OPEC countries who would be giving their own primary data. Of course, OPEC has a very rich and extensive history here in terms of collecting data from member states and monitoring the production levels.

Of course, what we are experiencing today is a new setup, a historic setup. We have 11 non-OPEC which have joined the efforts and this would call for establishing a new technical framework for collecting, analyzing, and monitoring the data. This means that for non-OPEC countries we would not just rely on second resources, but we would also be making extensive use of the primary data from these countries to supplement secondary resources.

The technical committee's objective is to collect, to analyze, and to present this data to the Joint Ministerial Monitoring Committee. We will plan on the final version of the report at the Joint Ministerial Monitoring Committee once it's ready to be distributed to all the members of OPEC and 11 Non-OPEC for assessment.

HE Novak: I would like to clarify what will be monitored?

We have agreed that the monitoring would be based on production data. The technical committee is free to use other indicators, including export of oil products to monitor the trends and the situation in the market in general. So of course, this is much broader analysis which the technical committee will be doing.

I would like to stress once again that the basic parameter which has been in the declaration of cooperation, is to monitor production, that is the supply and demand balance, and supply here means production of crude oil.

Energy intelligence: what would be an acceptable compliance rate? Is it 50%, 60%? Can we get some indication? Thank you.

HE Almarzooq: We have discussed this matter in our meeting and it was clear by all members of this committee, as well as the presidency of OPEC, that we will not accept anything less than 100 percent compliance.

Interfax: I would like to ask, Mr. Novak, you have mentioned that some countries are exceeding their plans in terms of production reduction. Could you give us more details and elaborate on these and name these countries, as well as by how much they are exceeding their obligations and what this may be connected to? Maybe this is linked in a way to Libya and Nigeria who are significantly overproducing and boosting their production?

HE Novak: At this point I, would like to say that there are still no final statistics for January. We are currently basing our assessment and analysis on statements and not final figures. Through indirect sources and indirect indication, we are seeing a significant stabilization of the market. We're seeing inventory draws. We are seeing volatility index drop and somewhat more promising pricing. These are all the results of the agreement's implementation.

We have seen His Excellence, Mr. Al-Falih statements from Saudi Arabia that the country has reduced output below the level which they had been producing in December.

I can also speak on behalf of the Russian Federation and that our reduction is significantly faster than our conservative assessments. Russian Federation have exceeded the initial plan base by a factor of more than two.

Of course, we do not have final data and data from all countries which are part of the cooperation declaration, but based on open sources, based on statements, and based on the data we have analyzed, we are estimating that the reduction in output as of now is close to 1.5 million barrels per day.

I would like to stress that this figure is only for the countries that we know the data. I believe that once we received the final statistics for January, we will all be positively surprised.

Trump wants to achieve energy independence from the literally OPEC cartel- What is OPEC Reaction?

February 2017 • Issue 2

Spanish News Agency: This is a question for Mr. Barkindo. I would like to know if you have any comments on the Energy Plan released by the White House, where it is said that President Trump wants to achieve energy independence from the literally OPEC cartel, if you have any reaction or any comment to this Energy Plan.

HE Barkindo: Thank you very much. We have also read online, like other online users, reports posted on the website of the White House, claiming to be the new energy policy of government. For OPEC as an organization, we will prefer to wait until the new energy secretary is sworn in and I am sure he would unveil the new energy policy of the US. Of course, as stakeholders in this global industry, we will also have our commentaries after, in-depth study and consultation within our governing bodies. Thank you.

Wall Street Journal: A question for Minister Novak. You described your reduction in production as significant, I am wondering if you had an actual number of the reduction so far. Thank you.

HE Novak: The average reduction in crude oil output from beginning of the year until now is somewhat above 100,000 barrels per day. This is significantly higher than our initial assessment of the technical capacity to reduce, which I would like to remind you, initially was a reduction of 50,000.

U.S. Shale production on the rise since agreement- does this help or hurt your goals

Bloomberg: since the agreement was announced on December the 10th, there has been an increase in US drilling activity and forecasting institutions have also increased their outlooks for US crude production, shale production for this year. Are you concerned at all, that the agreement and the resulting increase in prices is encouraging too much of a response in US shale? This may cause the surface to persist. Thank you.

HE Almarzooq: The increase in production, in conjunction with the increasing trend of prices is normal and is expected. The production level will depend on the cost of producing the shale oil in the US. Some areas are beyond the figures that we are looking at right now and some are below. So whenever the prices goes up, we expect the production to go up.

The cut that was made and hopefully we will continue,

I think it will cater for such increase in production, as well as increase in demand worldwide. So, we are not worried that the production of the US shale is increasing as prices goes because I think that will be consumed by the increasing demand as well.

I think our outgoing president has some thoughts on that as well, so I would like him to comment as well. Please.

HE Al-Sada: Thank you very much, Mr. Chairman. The demand is, as you can see, that it has always been healthy and for last year it was approximately an incremental increase of 1.2M. We do expect it to be in similar range this year. As you know, the number of drilling rigs have been increasing for the shale oil in the United States, but mind you, not all of them are meant to increase the production. You know that the shale oil and shale gas needs continuous drilling because of the nature of these wells, they produce for a year and a half or two and they drop in the production significantly. The drilling rigs must work continuously, first to continue the plateau. Second to increase the production.

I think with the increasing demand, eventually the shale oil will all be catered for as part of the demand portfolio worldwide. We will see, even with the increasing of the drilling rates in the shale gas, we are likely to see the balancing of the market. We have been seeing the trend going towards the balancing by the gradual but continuous drop in the commercial stock. That will continue and the rebalancing, which will be achieved later this year, is likely to happen when we are closing up to the five years average commercial stock. We see the trend and the trend is likely to continue. Thank you.

Press: I have a question for the Chairman of this conference and I would like to ask if the production data will be available to the public- and if yes; where can we find it?

HE Almarzooq: The data, as explained earlier by the co-chairman, His Excellency Mr. Novak is compiled from different sources, different agencies and these are all published data, from Platts, and Argus. However, the final data will be based on production data that will be compiled by the OPEC Secretariat.

Six Mega-Trends That Could Shape the Future of Energy

Ten years ago, the energy industry was focused on 'peak oil', while the shale gas revolution in the US had yet to start. As 2017 begins, what are the mega-trends that will shape the upcoming decades? Here, BP's head of long-term planning Dominic Emery identifies what lies ahead, from the rapid growth in renewables to changing demographics

1. Energy Transitions and The Dominant Fuel

BP's head of long-term planning Dominic Emery

Over time the energy sector experiences major transitions. For centuries, wood was the dominant fuel, then coal and now oil. As the 21st century develops, gas is now growing faster than any other fossil fuel - and renewables faster still.

With these changes in energy types, allied with sharp changes in prices, you have a complex scenario. The world is changing dramatically: from a supply and demand perspective, a geopolitical perspective and, importantly, from a climate policy perspective. The 2015 Paris agreement, which aims to keep the global temperature rise this century to well below 2°C, will dictate the speed of these transitions.

2. Oil supply

Over the past two decades, the energy world has moved from a situation where oil supply would peak and decline, to a situation where oil is so plentiful it has driven prices sharply downwards. That means a change in thinking is needed.

The focus is now much more around peak oil from a demand side; that there will be a period when demand for oil will peak and then gradually start to decline. Broad consensus suggests that this 'peak oil' window is most probably somewhere between 2025 and 2040, but there is considerable uncertainty surrounding this.

3. Gas supply

Natural gas resembles oil in being plentiful but differs in being used mainly for power and industry rather than transport. It has also tended to be traded within regions rather than across a single global market. However, this is changing - the amount of natural gas traded across borders is increasing as liquefied natural gas LNG surpasses pipeline imports as the dominant form of traded gas in the next 20 years.

As with oil, there is a lot of gas available very cheaply. Nowhere in our demand forecasts for the next few decades do we see gas peaking, unlike oil. Of course, from a carbon perspective, it has half the CO_2 emissions of coal when burnt to produce power.

4. Growth of Renewables

BP is preparing for a world where power comes increasingly from renewable sources. Wind and solar power have been growing faster than fossil fuels, although from a low base and with the benefit of government subsidies in many regions. Now, in many situations, they are becoming competitive with fossil fuels and are poised to deliver substantial shares of energy.

The growth of renewables has exceeded pretty much all forecasts. There has been double-digit growth for wind and solar in the past few years and because the manufacturing costs have come down as well, cost reductions have been about 80 per cent in solar and about 50 per cent in wind. However, what that ignores is the cost of intermittency because, of course, the sun does not shine all the time and the wind does not blow all the time. Therefore, in many places the existing grid and the existing fossil system are used to back up supply when energy from renewables is not available.

5. Electrification
The transport sector is set to change significantly, with electric vehicles, driverless - or autonomous - vehicles and new types of business.

I think there is no forecast anywhere that does not expect demand for electricity to grow and for electricity to become a more important part of the energy mix. There is also a sort of consumer desirability for newer electric vehicles, like the current Teslas, the new Tesla Model 3 that will be coming out at a much more competitive price and the BMW i8.

I think the interesting area is the combination of vehicle electrification with new methods of mobility, car-pooling and ride-sharing such as we are seeing with the likes of Hailo and Uber. And the impact of vehicle autonomy could be enormous but the uncertainty range is large.

6. Changes in demand
The demographics of emerging economies and the demands of millennials - those born post-1980 - are likely to change consumption and work patterns. In the older economies, patterns of demand are changing with the generations. *There is virtually no energy growth in the OECD Organization for Economic Cooperation and Development countries, particularly because of efficiency gains.*

Strong economic growth will mean the emerging economies - the non-OECD countries - are likely to account for nearly all the energy growth in the coming decades.

Then I think there are also the changing demands of the millennial generation. They are changing their consumption patterns and their working patterns. A lot of that will be enabled more digitally than in the past, and in ways that we possibly have not even thought of yet.

President Trump Orders revive Keystone XL Pipeline, Dakota Access pipelines and Advance Energy Infrastructure Projects

In keeping with his promise to reduce the burden of regulations and expedite high priority energy and infrastructure projects that will create jobs and increase national security; President Donald J. Trump has signed a series of Executive Orders and Presidential Memoranda.

Presidential Memorandum Regarding Construction of the Keystone XL Pipeline

With this Presidential Memorandum, President Trump will help fulfill the campaign promise of initiating the process for approving the Keystone XL Pipeline.

The Keystone XL Pipeline is an 1,100-mile crude oil pipeline to connect oil production in Alberta, Canada to refineries in the United States.

Construction and operation of the Keystone XL Pipeline, as well as oil production and refining activities related to it, would create tens of thousands of jobs for American workers, enhance our nation's energy security, support affordable and reliable energy for American families, and generate significant State and local tax revenues that can be invested in schools, hospitals, and infrastructure.

Presidential Memorandum Regarding Construction of the Dakota Access Pipeline

With this Presidential

President Donald J. Trump

Memorandum, President Trump directed the relevant Federal agencies, including the Army Corps of Engineers, to expedite reviews and approvals for the remaining portions of

February 2017 • Issue 2

the Dakota Access Pipeline., a $3.8 billion, 1,100-mile pipeline designed to carry around 500,000 barrels per day of crude oil from the Bakken and Three Forks oil production areas in North Dakota to oil markets in the U.S.

Now, DAPL is more than 90 percent complete across its entire route. Only a limited stretch of the project is not yet constructed. Timely review and approval of energy pipelines is critical to a strong economy, energy independence, and national security.

Presidential Memorandum Regarding Construction of American Pipelines

In keeping with his commitment to "Buy American, Hire American", President Trump directed the Secretary of Commerce, in consultation with all relevant executive departments and agencies, to develop a plan under which all new pipelines, as well as retrofitted, repaired, or expanded pipelines, inside the borders of the United States, including portions of pipelines, use materials and equipment produced in the United States, to the maximum extent possible and to the extent permitted by law. The Secretary shall submit the plan to the President within 180 days of the date of this memorandum.

Presidential Memorandum Streamlining Permitting and Reducing Regulatory Burdens for Domestic Manufacturing

With this Presidential Memorandum, President Trump helps fulfill the campaign promise of boosting domestic manufacturing by determining a plan of action for expediting approvals for manufacturing and reducing regulatory burdens.

Under this Presidential Memorandum, the Secretary of Commerce will conduct outreach to stakeholders and solicit comments from the public concerning Federal actions to streamline permitting and reduce regulatory burdens affecting domestic manufacturers.

The Commerce Secretary will submit a report to the President identifying recommendations to streamline Federal permitting processes for domestic manufacturing and to reduce regulatory burdens affecting domestic manufacturers. The report should identify priority actions as well as recommended deadlines for completing actions.

Executive Order Expediting Environmental Reviews and Approvals for High Priority Infrastructure Projects

With this Executive Order, President Trump will establish a framework for expediting environmental reviews for high priority infrastructure projects.

Delays and other inefficiencies in the environmental review and permitting process are severely impeding critically important projects to rebuild and modernize our nation's infrastructure, such as highways, bridges, tunnels, the electrical grid, ports, water systems, airports, railways and pipelines.

Per one study, the U S antiquated power rigs waste the equivalent of 200 coal-fired power plants, water pipes leak trillions of gallons of water, and gridlock on roads and railroads wastes hundreds of billions annually.

Stakeholders Reactions:

U.S. Sen. Lisa Murkowski, R-Alaska, "President Trump recognizes the importance of energy infrastructure, and that is a welcome sign. We need a president who understands the significant contributions that infrastructure makes to our economy and our national security," Murkowski said. "I support consultation with the people affected by infrastructure projects, and we must ensure that they are built and operated responsibly. However, for too long federal agencies have been sources of unnecessary delay and uncertainty. Reform is long overdue, and the president's actions are a good start."

API President and CEO Jack Gerard, "We are pleased to see the new direction being taken by this administration to recognize the importance of our nation's energy infrastructure by restoring the rule of law in the permitting process that's critical to pipelines and other infrastructure projects," said Gerard. "Critical energy infrastructure projects like the Keystone XL and the Dakota Access Pipelines will help deliver energy to American consumers and businesses safely and efficiently.

"The United States is leading the world in the production and refining of oil and natural gas and in the reduction of carbon emissions which are near 20-year lows. We look forward to working with the Trump administration on putting in place policies to continue our nation's energy leadership that will benefit American consumers and workers, while protecting the environment."

The American Council for Capital Formation, "In signing

the Keystone XL and Dakota Access executive orders, President Trump is following through on his campaign promise to reverse the previous administration's approach of abusing the regulatory process to pursue a political agenda. Unfortunately, that agenda came at the expense of the U.S. economy and American jobs. The action by President Trump not only respects the rule of law, it also signals that America is once again open for business. Investment, growth and job creation should be the cornerstone of the President's agenda and the executive orders reflect that commitment.

"Over the past several years, the United States has reemerged as the world's leading energy producer. Unfortunately, our infrastructure has not kept pace and additional economic growth has been held back by a lack of pipelines and other energy infrastructure that have become the targets of special interest groups. Basic infrastructure projects like Keystone XL and Dakota Access pipelines – and the economic activity and jobs that accompany them – are long overdue.

"The American Council for Capital Formation is pleased that the new administration has revisited these two important projects and taken a pro-growth approach to our nation's energy sector."

PHMSA Final Rule Amends HMR to Maintain Consistency with International Regulations

The U.S. Department of Transportation's DOT Pipeline and Hazardous Materials Safety Administration PHMSA has placed on public inspection a final rule that amends the U.S. Hazardous Material Regulations HMR to maintain consistency with international regulations and standards. The amendments to the HMR include changes to proper shipping names; hazard classes; packing groups; special provisions; packaging authorizations; air transport quantity limitations; and vessel stowage requirements.

The revisions harmonize the HMR with recent changes in the International Maritime Dangerous Goods Code, the International Civil Aviation Organization's Technical Instructions for the Safe Transport of Dangerous Goods by Air, and the United Nations Recommendations on the Transport of Dangerous Goods—Model Regulations. In addition, several amendments resulted from coordination with Canada under the U.S.-Canada Regulatory Cooperation Council. Prior to adoption, PHMSA considers each amendment on its own merit; PHMSA seeks to promote consistency without diminishing transportation safety or imposing undue burden on the regulatory community. The final rule is effective January 18, 2017. Mandatory compliance begins January 1, 2018, unless otherwise specified.

PHMSA Final Rule Requires Faster Notification Following Pipeline Accidents

The U.S. Department of Transportation's Pipeline and Hazardous Materials Safety Administration PHMSA has issued a final rule entitled, "Operator Qualification, Cost Recovery, Accident and Incident Notification, and Other Pipeline Safety Changes." Specifically, the rulemaking lays out a specific time frame requirement for telephonic or electronic notifications of accidents and incidents.

The rule also amends drug and alcohol testing requirements, and incorporates consensus standards by reference for in-line inspection and Stress Corrosion Cracking Direct Assessment. The rule addresses mandates included in the Pipeline Safety, Regulatory Certainty, and Job Creation Act of 2011. The rulemaking is scheduled to publish in the Federal Register on January 23, 2017 and is currently on public inspection. The rulemaking will become effective 60 days from the date of its publication.

Synthetic Genomics and ExxonMobil Renew Algae Biofuels Research Agreement

- Renewal continues fundamental research into advanced biofuels
- Large team of researchers focused on Synthetic Genomics' core synthetic biology technologies
- Progress continues toward development of algae-based transportation fuels

Synthetic Genomics, Inc. and ExxonMobil has announced that they have extended their agreement to conduct joint research into advanced algae biofuels after making significant progress in understanding algae genetics, growth characteristics and increasing oil production.

ExxonMobil and Synthetic Genomics have been jointly researching and developing oil from algae for use as a renewable, lower-emission alternative to traditional transportation fuels since launching the program in 2009. Work continues toward developing strains of algae that demonstrate significantly improved photosynthetic efficiency and oil production through selection and genetic engineering of higher-performance algae strains. The agreement continues to focus on Synthetic Genomics' core strengths in synthetic biology and builds on recent discoveries of biological pathways regulating lipid production and growth in advanced algal strains.

"Together with ExxonMobil, we have made significant strides to identify and enhance algal strains capable of high oil production while still maintaining desirable rates of growth," said Oliver Fetzer, Ph.D., chief executive officer of Synthetic Genomics. "The extension of our agreement reflects the tremendous progress made to date, and the promise in using our core synthetic biology technologies to build cell production systems capable of reshaping industries."

Vijay Swarup, vice president for research and development at ExxonMobil Research and Engineering Company, said that renewal of the agreement underscores the importance of the research and recognition of milestones the team has achieved together over the past few years.

"Synthetic Genomics and ExxonMobil remain committed to advancing the scientific fundamentals of algal biofuels," Swarup said. "We know this will be a long-term endeavor and are optimistic based on the results we have seen to date."

The development of algae biofuels and a path toward commercial-scale production remain key components of ExxonMobil's suite of research projects focused on producing energy to meet global demand while reducing greenhouse gas emissions to mitigate the risk of climate change.

ExxonMobil is engaged in a broad range of research on advanced biofuels, partnering with universities and other companies. The purpose of these research and development programs is to explore new technologies and seek the best pathways toward scalable and cost-effective production of advanced biofuels.

Global demand for transportation fuels is projected to rise by nearly 30 percent through 2040, and accelerating the reduction in emissions from the transportation sector will play a critical role in reducing global greenhouse gas emissions.

ExxonMobil to Acquire Companies Doubling Permian Basin Resource to 6 Billion Barrels

- Companies' assets include 250,000 acres in highly prolific Permian Basin
- Adds more than 3.4 billion barrels of oil equivalent, of which 75 percent is liquids
- Upfront acquisition cost of $5.6 billion to be paid in ExxonMobil shares

Exxon Mobil Corporation said that it will more than double its Permian Basin resource to 6 billion barrels of oil equivalent through the acquisition of companies owned by the Bass family of Fort Worth, Texas, with an estimated resource of 3.4 billion barrels of oil equivalent in New Mexico's Delaware Basin, a highly prolific, oil-prone section of the Permian Basin.

ExxonMobil will make an upfront payment of $5.6 billion in ExxonMobil shares, and a series of additional contingent cash payments totaling up to $1 billion, to be paid beginning in 2020 and ending no later than 2032 commensurate with the development of the resource.

Darren W. Woods, ExxonMobil chairman and chief executive officer, said the high-quality properties are a major addition to ExxonMobil's unconventional liquids portfolio managed by its subsidiary, XTO Energy Inc.

"This acquisition strengthens ExxonMobil's significant presence in the dominant U.S. growth area for onshore oil production," said Woods. "This investment gives us an exceptional Delaware Basin position in a proven multi-stacked play that can generate attractive returns in a low-price environment.

"The highly-contiguous position will provide significant cost advantages in developing 3.4 billion barrels of resource, of which 75 percent is liquids. By utilizing ExxonMobil's technological strength coupled with its unconventional development capabilities we can drill the longest lateral wells in the Permian Basin, reducing development costs and increasing reserve capture."

The acquired companies, which include the operating entity BOPCO, hold about 275,000 acres of leasehold, and production of more than 18,000 net oil equivalent barrels per day, about 70 percent of which is liquids. This includes about 250,000 acres of leasehold in the Permian Basin, the bulk of that in contiguous, held-by-production units in the New Mexico Delaware Basin, with more than 60 billion barrels of oil equivalent estimated in place. The companies also hold producing acreage in other areas in the United States.

ExxonMobil is producing approximately 140,000 net oil-equivalent barrels per day across its Permian Basin leasehold.

Shell to Sell Stake in Sadaf Chemicals Joint Venture in Saudi Arabia to Sabic

Shell and SABIC have signed an agreement whereby SABIC will acquire Shell's 50 per cent share in the petrochemicals SADAF joint venture, located in Jubail, Kingdom of Saudi Arabia for $820 million. The SADAF joint venture encompasses six world-scale petrochemical plants with a total output of more than 4 million metric tons per year. This announcement marks an early termination of the joint venture agreement which was due to expire in 2020.

This acquisition will enable SABIC to further optimize operations at SADAF and further invest in the facilities, integrating them with SABICs other affiliates. This step will allow Shell to focus its downstream activities and make selective investments to support the growth of its global chemicals business.

Graham van't Hoff, Executive Vice President Chemicals,

Shell, said: "Our partnership with SABIC, spanning more than thirty years, has been a great success story. We're proud to have established together one of the first petrochemical ventures in Saudi Arabia - it has grown substantially since the start, in 1986. We will continue to explore potential future opportunities with SABIC."

Yousef Al-Benyan, SABIC Vice chairman and CEO, said, "Since SABIC's early days, we have enjoyed a strong relationship with Shell Chemicals. We are confident that our journey of partnership together will continue and grow in strength. With this transaction SABIC is looking to capitalize on synergy opportunities of SADAF with other affiliates, and improve its operation and profitability."

The transaction is subject to regulatory approval and is expected to complete later this year. Shell's other activities in the country are not impacted.

USA Oil and Gas Monitor
For Daily News Report and Analysis • www.usaoilandgasmonitor.com

BP to Sell Part of Interests in Magnus Field and Sullom Voe Terminal in UK North Sea to EnQuest

BP has announced it has agreed to sell part of its interests in the Magnus oil field and some associated pipeline infrastructure in the UK northern North Sea and in the Sullom Voe Terminal SVT on Shetland to EnQuest.

Included in the agreement are: 25 per cent of BP's 100 per cent stake in Magnus, 25 per cent of BP's interests in several associated pipelines and a 3 per cent interest in the Sullom Voe Terminal from BP Exploration Operating Company Limited's BPEOC current total 12 per cent stake. The sale price of $85 million is expected to be met by EnQuest from the sharing of future cash flows from the assets and the agreement will not include any upfront payment to BP.

Subject to partner, regulatory and other third party approvals, operatorship of both Magnus and SVT will transfer from BP to EnQuest on completion. The sale will not affect BP's rights to capacity in SVT.

Under the terms of the agreement, EnQuest has an option, exercisable between 1 July 2018 and 15 January 2019, to purchase BP's remaining 75 per cent interest in Magnus, a further 9 per cent interest in SVT and the remainder of BP's interests in the associated pipelines for a consideration of $300 million. Under this option, after the recovery of consideration and adjustments, BP would also retain 50 per cent of net cash flows from these assets, up to a limit of $1 billion. The consideration for this further acquisition would be met by EnQuest through a mixture of cash and future asset cash flows.

BP group chief executive Bob Dudley commented: "EnQuest's experience of investing in and extending the life of mature assets in the North Sea make them a natural operator of Magnus and Sullom Voe in this later phase of their life. We believe this will enable them to prolong the life of the assets, benefiting the region and creating additional value for both EnQuest and BP shareholders. In addition to investing in and growing our core businesses, BP will continue to seek innovative opportunities such as this to work with partners to maximize value creation from our entire portfolio."

Mark Thomas, BP North Sea Regional President said: "In recent years, we have been focusing our North Sea portfolio around core assets west of Shetland and in the central North Sea - bringing new fields into production, redeveloping and renewing existing producing facilities, acquiring new acreage and interests through license rounds and farm-ins and selling some of our mature assets to those who see greater strategic fit with their businesses. Sullom Voe and Magnus have been great businesses for BP, but to maximize the economic life of these important assets, we believe this deal will offer them a better long-term future.

"With their integrated skills, operational scale, cost structures and high levels of operating efficiency we have seen what EnQuest can do on the Thistle, Deveron and Don fields that were previously operated by BP. We believe this is a good example of having the right assets in the right hands, offering new opportunities for the assets and benefitting the UKCS, in the spirit of Maximizing Economic Recovery 'MER UK'."

Oil production from the BP-operated Clair field will continue to be exported through SVT, and the new Clair Ridge development will also export oil to the terminal when it comes on-stream. Gas produced from the Foinaven and Clair fields will also continue to be processed through SVT. Gas from the re-developed Schiehallion and Loyal fields will export to SVT when they are brought back into production in the coming months.

SVT and Magnus are expected to transition to EnQuest as fully operational entities, with those staff who operate and support the assets expected to transfer with the businesses. Their contractual terms and conditions are protected under UK Transfer of Undertakings TUPE regulations. Around 100 BP staff are currently associated with Magnus and associated infrastructure and approximately 240 with SVT. BP

will now begin consultation with in scope staff.

Subject to the receipt of regulatory and other third party approvals, BP aims to complete the sale and transfer of operatorship during 2017.

The deal comprises:

- The sale of 25 per cent of BP's 100 per cent interest in the Magnus field, including the transfer of operatorship:
  - BP will retain the remaining 75 per cent of the Magnus field as a non-operating co-owner
- The sale of 25 per cent of BP Exploration Operating Company Limited's BPEOC's 12 per cent interest in SVT, including the transfer of operatorship subject to partner and regulatory approval:
  - BPEOC will retain 9 per cent of SVT as a non-operating owner
  - BP will also retain 4.4 per cent of SVT through Britoil
- The sale of 25 per cent of BP's interests in associated pipeline systems:
  - 9 per cent from BP's 36 per cent interest in the Northern Leg Gas Pipeline NLGP, including the transfer of operatorship
  - 3.83 per cent from BP's 15.32 per cent interest in the Ninian Pipeline System NPS, including transfer of operatorship
- Production from Magnus averaged around 17,000 barrels of oil equivalent per day gross during 2016
- The sale will not impact BP's rights to capacity in SVT
- BP is continuing to invest in its major projects west of

Shetland, Clair Ridge and Quad204, both of which will bring important new oil into production

- BP is also investing significantly in the reliability and integrity of existing assets through an extensive renewal program. It recently completed a Magnus life extension program and is nearing completion of a £670m investment in the ETAP cluster of fields which is expected to extend its future until at least 2035
- Over the next 18 months, BP plans to participate in up to five exploration wells in the UK in addition to drilling approximately 50 development wells over the next 3-4 years
- BP was awarded 12 license blocks across the northern and central North Sea as part of last year's 28th licensing round and has participated strongly in the 29th round

Data Highlights
WTI crude oil futures price
1/25/2017: $52.75/barrels
up $1.67 from week earlier
up $21.30 from year earlier
Natural gas futures price
1/25/2017: $3.332/MMBtu
up $0.030 from week earlier
up $1.152 from year earlier
Natural gas inventories
1/20/2017: 2,798 Bcf
down 119 Bcf from week earlier
down 348 Bcf from year earlier
Crude oil inventories
1/20/2017: 488.3 million barrels
up 2.8 million barrels from week earlier
up 24.7 million barrels from year earlier
Weekly coal production
1/21/2017: 16.759 million tons
up 1.043 million tons from week earlier
up 2.858 million tons from year earlier

February 2017 • Issue 2

Canadian Court Rejects Attempt to Enforce Fraudulent Ecuadorian Judgment Against Chevron Subsidiary

A Canadian court has ruled that the fraudulent Ecuadorian judgment against Chevron Corporation cannot be enforced against Chevron Canada Limited, an indirect subsidiary. The court found that Chevron Canada Limited is a separate entity from Chevron Corporation, not a party to the Ecuadorian lawsuit and not a debtor to the judgment. In its decision, the court stated, "Chevron Corporation and Chevron Canada are separate legal entities with separate rights and obligations." Thus, the court found that "plaintiffs' claim cannot succeed against Chevron Canada" and dismissed the claim against it.

In a related ruling, the court also rejected an attempt by the plaintiffs to prohibit Chevron Corporation from using the extensive evidence of fraud committed by the plaintiffs as part of the company's defense against the recognition and enforcement action in Canada.

"Once again, the plaintiffs' attempts to enforce their fraudulent judgment have been rebuked," said R. Hewitt Pate, vice president and general counsel, Chevron Corporation. "We are confident that any jurisdiction that examines the facts of this case and the misconduct committed by the plaintiffs will find the Ecuadorian judgment illegitimate and unenforceable."

In its decision, the Canadian court referenced the 2014 U.S. federal court decision, which found that a judgment issued against Chevron Corporation by a court in Ecuador was the product of fraud and racketeering activity, including extortion, money laundering, wire fraud, witness tampering and obstruction of justice. The U.S. court also prohibited the Ecuadorian judgment from being enforced in the United States. This decision was unanimously affirmed by the United States Court of Appeals for the Second Circuit in 2016, which stated that Donziger and his team engaged in a "parade of corrupt actions...including coercion, fraud and bribery."

Because Chevron Corporation has no assets in Ecuador, the plaintiffs, led by American attorney Steven Donziger, are attempting to enforce the fraudulent judgment in other jurisdictions, including Canada, Argentina and Brazil. In Canada, Donziger and his team were seeking to enforce the judgment against both Chevron Corporation, which has no assets in Canada, and Chevron Canada Limited, which is not a party to the Ecuadorian lawsuit. Today's decision prevents them from pursuing Chevron Canada Limited's assets.

The Ecuadorian judgment is being questioned in other jurisdictions as well. In 2015, Brazil's Federal Prosecutor's Office issued a recommendation to the country's Superior Court of Justice that the judgment not be recognized for enforcement, finding that it was "issued irregularly, especially under uncontested acts of corruption" and that recognizing it would violate Brazilian and "international public order." Similarly, in 2016, Argentina's public prosecutor's office recommended that its National Court reject the effort to recognize the Ecuadorian judgment in that country.

Global Crude Oil Balances Expected to Tighten Through 2018

EIA estimates that crude oil and other liquids inventories grew by 2.0 million barrels per day in the fourth quarter of 2016, driven by an increase in production and a significant, but seasonal, drop in consumption. Global production and consumption are both projected to increase through 2018, but consumption is expected to increase at a faster rate than production. Thus, global balances are expected to tighten.

The production increase in the fourth quarter of 2016 largely reflects members of the Organization of the Petroleum Exporting Countries OPEC ramping up production in advance of implementing the November agreement on production cuts. Global production is expected to have increased by 1.6 million b/d in the fourth quarter of 2016, with OPEC accounting for 0.9 million b/d, or 55 percent, of this increase. EIA estimates that total global production averaged 96.4 million b/d in 2016. Global production is expected to increase to 97.5 million b/d in 2017 and to 98.9 million b/d in 2018.

The large seasonal consumption declines in the fourth quarter of 2016 are not expected to continue as global consumption of petroleum and liquids is forecast to grow at a faster rate than production through 2018. Annual petroleum and liquids consumption for 2016 is estimated at 95.6 million b/d and is forecast to increase to 97.2 million b/d in 2017 and 98.7 million b/d in 2018. On a quarterly basis, consumption is expected to be greater than production in the third quarter of both 2017 and 2018, leading to stock draws in both periods.

Global inventories are expected to have increased an average of 0.9 million b/d in 2016. The January 2017 Short-Term Energy Outlook forecasts annual crude oil balances to tighten over the next two years, with 2017 averaging a 0.3 million b/d stock build and 2018 averaging a 0.1 million b/d stock build. By the second half of 2018, inventories are expected to decline by an average of 0.1 million b/d.

With annual inventory builds, along with a lack of a significant draw on existing inventories, prices remain below $60/b through the end of 2018. Brent crude oil spot prices are expected to remain flat during 2017, in part because of the responsiveness of U.S. tight oil production to rising oil prices in late 2016, and they are expected to average $53/b for the year. EIA forecasts Brent prices will slowly increase in 2018, beginning the year at $54/b in January and ending the year at $59/b in December, averaging $56/b annually.

Federal Revenues from Energy on Federal Lands Declined In 2016 Due to Low Oil Prices

In fiscal year 2016, the U.S. government collected almost $6 billion in revenues from royalties, rental costs, and other fees from activities related to energy production on federal and American Indian lands, per the Department of Interior's Office of Natural Resource Revenue. These activities include the production of coal, oil, natural gas, and hydrocarbon gas liquids HGLs as well as, more recently, renewables.

From FY2010 to FY2013, federal

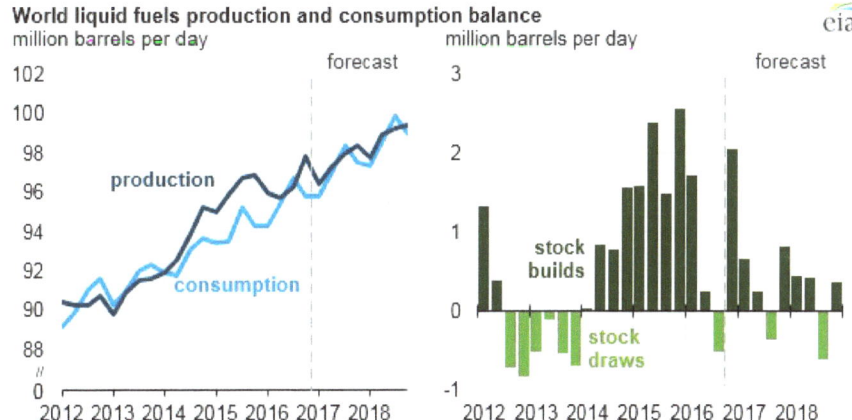

World liquid fuels production and consumption balance
million barrels per day

revenues increased, driven by growth in offshore and onshore revenue during a time of relatively high oil prices. Revenues in FY2013 exceeded $14 billion and have since decreased in each successive year. Revenues in FY2016 were the lowest since at least FY2004.

Royalties accounted for 86 percent of total FY2016 revenue $5.1 billion from energy production on federal lands. Royalties are based on the amount of a resource produced and its value. As prices change, royalty revenue also fluctuates.

Royalties from crude oil accounted for 55 percent of the total revenue collected by the U.S. government from activities related to energy production on federal lands from FY2010 to FY2016. Despite growing oil production, revenue has decreased since FY2014 as the price of oil has fallen along with the valuation used to determine royalties. Natural gas, including hydrocarbon gas liquids in the raw natural gas stream, made up an additional 20 percent of total revenue since 2010, and decreases in the price of natural gas since early 2014 also affecting total royalties. Royalties from coal production contributed an average of 7 percent of total revenues over this period.

Most of the remaining revenue came from rent on leases of public land paid annually, fees, and bonuses a one-time payment paid

upon winning a bid, mostly from production of fossil fuels. Royalties and rents from other resources, which includes renewables like geothermal generation and wind energy, were about 1 percent of total revenue from 2010 through 2016.

Federal royalties collected from energy production are distributed among federal, state, and other funds. In FY2016, the U.S. Treasury was the largest recipient, receiving $2.4 billion. States also receive a share from onshore production and offshore production based on the activities occurring in each state. Thirty-seven states collectively received almost $1.32 billion in revenue sharing in 2016. More than half a billion dollars $560 million was disbursed to 34 federally recognized American Indian tribes and more than 35,000 individual Indian mineral owners.

The remaining $2.8 billion went to two dedicated funds: $1.01 billion to the Reclamation Fund, which is used for water management and efficiency programs for the benefit of 17 western states, and $884 million to the Land and Water Conservation Fund, which provides grants to governments at all levels for easements, land acquisition, and overall conservation. The Historic Preservation Fund, which had received $150 million annually, expired at the end of FY2015.

www.ingramcontent.com/pod-product-compliance
Lightning Source LLC
Chambersburg PA
CBHW060812290526
45792CB00005BA/1617